WATER

SUPER COOL
SCIENCE
EXPERIMENTS:
WATER

by Charnan Simon and Ariel Kazunas

CHERRY LAKE PUBLISHING • ANN ARBOR, MICHIGAN

CHERRY LAKE
Publishing

A NOTE TO PARENTS AND TEACHERS: Please review the instructions for these experiments before your children do them. Be sure to help them with any experiments you do not think they can safely conduct on their own.

A NOTE TO KIDS: Be sure to ask an adult for help with these experiments when you need it. Always put your safety first!

Published in the United States of America by
Cherry Lake Publishing
Ann Arbor, Michigan
www.cherrylakepublishing.com

Content Editor: Robert Wolffe, EdD,
Professor of Teacher Education,
Bradley University, Peoria, Illinois

Book design and illustration: The Design Lab

Grateful acknowledgment to Deborah Simon, Department of Chemistry,
Whitman College

Photo Credits: Cover and page 1, ©Bcreigh/Dreamstime.com; page
4, ©iStockphoto.com/mrloz; page 5, ©Juriah Mosin, used under
license from Shutterstock, Inc.; page 8, ©Autayeu/Dreamstime.com;
page 12, ©iStockphoto.com/travellinglight; page 16, ©iStockphoto.
com/RyersonClark; page 20, ©iStockphoto.com/Spanic; page 24,
©iStockphoto.com/ericfoltz; page 28, ©iStockphoto.com/Kemter

Library of Congress Cataloging-in-Publication Data
Simon, Charnan.
  Super cool science experiments: Water / by Charnan Simon and
Ariel Kazunas.
      p. cm.—(Science explorer)
  Includes bibliographical references and index.
  ISBN-13: 978-1-60279-529-7   ISBN-10: 1-60279-529-0 (lib. bdg.)
  ISBN-13: 978-1-60279-608-9   ISBN-10: 1-60279-608-4 (pbk.)
  1. Water—Experiments—Juvenile literature. 2. Vapors—Juvenile
literature. 3. Hydrology—Juvenile literature. I. Kazunas, Ariel.
II. Title. III. Title: Water. IV. Title. V. Series.
QD169.W3S45 2010
  546'.22078—dc22   2009008082

Cherry Lake Publishing would like to acknowledge the work
of The Partnership for 21st Century Skills. Please visit
www.21stcenturyskills.org for more information.

WATER

TABLE OF CONTENTS

What Makes a Scientist?

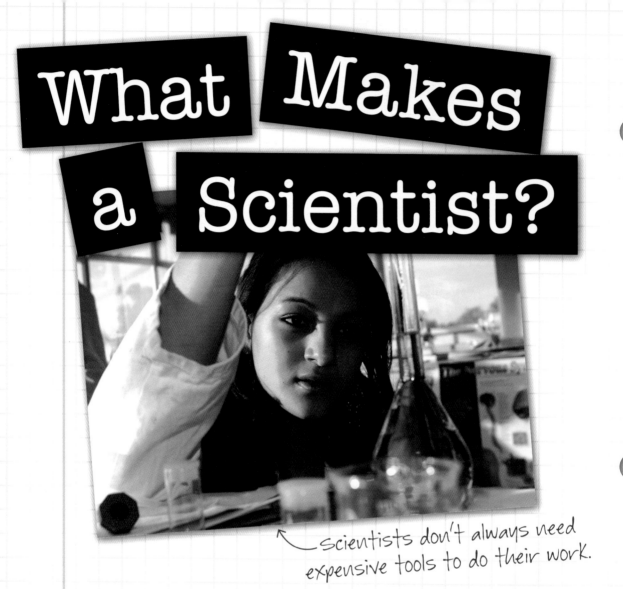

~ Scientists don't always need expensive tools to do their work.

Have you ever wondered what it takes to be a scientist? Do you think you could be one? Scientists like to do experiments to test answers to their questions. Did you know you can do experiments using things you have at home? In this book, we'll see how scientists think by doing experiments with water. We'll even learn how to design our own experiments. Let's have some fun as we discover what makes a scientist!

First Things First

Scientists learn by studying things in nature very carefully. For example, scientists who study water know it can change forms. They see that some things float on water while other things sink. They do experiments to see how and why this happens.

You can learn about water by exploring nature.

Good scientists take notes on everything they discover. They write down their observations. Sometimes those observations lead scientists to ask new questions. With new questions in mind, they design experiments to find the answers.

When scientists design experiments, they must think very clearly. The way they think about problems is often called the scientific method. What is the scientific method? It's a step-by-step way of finding answers to specific questions. The steps don't always follow the same pattern. Sometimes scientists change their minds. The process often works something like this:

Scientific method →

- **Step One:** A scientist gathers the facts and makes observations about one particular thing.
- **Step Two:** The scientist comes up with a question that is not answered by all the observations and facts.
- **Step Three:** The scientist creates a hypothesis. This is a statement of what the scientist thinks is probably the answer to the question.
- **Step Four:** The scientist tests the hypothesis. He or she designs an experiment to see whether the hypothesis is correct. The scientist does the experiment and writes down what happens.
- **Step Five:** The scientist draws a conclusion based on how the experiment turned out. The conclusion might be that the hypothesis is correct. Sometimes, though, the hypothesis is not correct. In that case, the scientist might develop a new hypothesis and another experiment.

In the following experiments, we'll see the scientific method in action. First, we'll gather some facts and observations about water. For each experiment, we'll develop a question and a hypothesis. Next, we'll do an actual experiment to see if our hypothesis is correct. By the end of the experiment, we should know something new about water. Scientists, are you ready? Let's get started!

Let's dive in to some water experiments!

Experiment #1
Thin Skin

Have you ever watched water drops drip from a faucet?

What do you already know about water? Have you seen water form drops when it rains or when a faucet is leaking? Did you know that's because water molecules hang on to each other?

Molecules are the smallest parts of a substance that still have the chemical properties of that substance. Water molecules pull on the molecules all around them. If there aren't any molecules above them because they're on the top of a lake or the outside of a raindrop, the water molecules pull even harder on the ones next to and below them. This causes the surface of the liquid to act like a skin, a result that is called surface tension. Some insects use surface tension to walk across water!

These observations lead us to some questions. Is it possible to change surface tension? Could we do this by adding something to water? Let's work on an experiment to find out. Our hypothesis can be: **Adding other molecules to water makes it harder for the water molecules to stick together.**

Here's what you'll need:
- 2 clear cups or glasses
- A spoon
- A bowl of water
- Liquid dishwashing soap
- A small loop of thread

Gather your materials before you begin the experiment.

Add water slowly and watch what happens.

Instructions:

1. Fill a glass almost to the rim with water. Place it on a flat surface.
2. Use the spoon to add water from the bowl slowly to the glass. Try to get the water to bulge up and over the rim of the glass without spilling. This is surface tension at work!
3. Now, carefully drop a bit of liquid soap on the top of your glass of water. Record what happens. Does this support your hypothesis? Why?

4. Fill the second glass with water, but not quite as high. Dampen a small loop of thread. Place it on top of the water in the glass. Write down your observations. What does the thread loop look like?
5. Put a drop of dishwashing soap in the middle of the loop. Don't let any soap touch the thread or the water outside of the loop. Watch carefully and record your observations.

Conclusion:
What did you learn about how soap affects surface tension? Soap reduces surface tension. That explains what happened to the water in the first glass when you added the soap. Adding soap to the inside of the thread loop in the second glass weakened the surface tension in that area. Soap molecules have properties that make it difficult for water molecules to stick together. This makes it harder for the water to keep the flexible "skin" on the surface.

Was the water pulling harder on the inside or the outside of the loop? How does this explain what happens to the loop's shape? The surface tension outside the loop doesn't change because it did not come into contact with the soap. So this tension surrounding the loop pulled on the string. Did our experiment support our hypothesis?

Experiment #2
Will It Sink or Float?

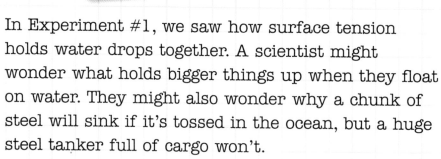

Did you ever wonder how a ship this big and heavy can float?

In Experiment #1, we saw how surface tension holds water drops together. A scientist might wonder what holds bigger things up when they float on water. They might also wonder why a chunk of steel will sink if it's tossed in the ocean, but a huge steel tanker full of cargo won't.

Before we come up with a hypothesis, we need a little more scientific background information. Density is how heavy or light something is for its size. Keep in mind that a small object that seems light can still be dense. When an object displaces something, it takes the place of something else. How do you think density and displacement relate to floating and sinking?

We need a new hypothesis: **If an object is too dense, it will sink. But an object that can displace enough water will float.**

Here's what you'll need:
- 2 sheets of the same amount of aluminum foil
- A large measuring cup or mixing bowl
- Water
- Some coins, pebbles, or glass marbles

Look around your house for small objects.

Instructions:

1. Crumple 1 sheet of aluminum foil into a tight, solid ball. Shape the other sheet into a boat with sides.

2. Fill about ⅔ of your bowl with water.

3. Drop the aluminum ball into the water. See what happens and write down your observations.

4. Take the ball out, and put the boat in the water. What happens? Is it what you expected?

5. Take your boat out of the water, and drop in some of your coins, pebbles, or marbles. What happens? Why do you think this is?

6. Remove the coins, pebbles, and marbles and put the boat back in the water. One by one, begin placing the coins, pebbles, or marbles in the boat. What happens? How many objects can the boat support before it sinks?

You need to build an aluminum foil boat.

Conclusion:

We know that objects denser than water will sink.

But you used exactly the same material for the ball and the boat. So why did the ball sink and the boat float? That's where shape comes into play. When you shaped the boat, you made an object that spread out across the surface of the water. It covered a larger surface than the ball. The boat displaced more water.

Volume is the amount of space taken up by an object. Objects float when they weigh less than the volume of water they displace. As you added objects to the boat, it eventually began to sink. When the boat had too many objects in it, it weighed more than the amount of water it pushed aside. When that happened, the boat sank. Was your hypothesis correct? Why? Write down your conclusions.

If you fill two similar containers all the way up with water, they will weigh the same. Suppose you drop a wooden block into one of the containers. Which one do you think will weigh more? Think about how things float. What does the block have to do to stay on top of the water? It pushes aside its weight in water over the sides of the container. Both containers will still weigh exactly the same!

What if you fill the containers with only a small amount of water? Will there still be enough water for the block to push aside, or will it touch the bottom? If there isn't enough water to push out of the container, does this mean the container will weigh more? Or will both containers still weigh the same? Why or why not?

Experiment #3
Water, Water Everywhere!

You've probably seen water vapor rising from a pot of boiling water.

Now let's consider water vapor, or water in its gas state. Water vapor is almost always in the air around you, even when you can't see or feel it. Have you ever seen the bathroom mirror steam up after you take a hot shower? Or a window fog up after you breathe on it, especially in the winter? That's the water vapor in the air and in your breath when it condenses, or turns back into a liquid.

What causes this change? What's the difference between the air after a hot shower and the surface of the mirror? What's the difference between your breath and the surface of the window? Could it have something to do with temperature? Our hypothesis is: **When water vapor cools, it changes back into a liquid.**

Here's what you'll need:

- 2 clean, dry glasses (one must be microwave safe)
- A freezer
- A microwave
- A room that's not too hot or too cold

Be sure to record your observations.

Observations

Instructions:

1. Put a glass in the freezer for 1 minute.
2. Then heat the microwave-safe glass in the microwave for 1 minute. Keep the first glass in the freezer in the meantime.
3. When the microwave minute is up, take the first glass out of the freezer and the second glass out of the microwave. Handle them very carefully. Place the glasses next to each other on the counter. Make sure they don't touch each other.
4. Wait 1 minute. Record what you see.

Conclusion:

Did anything happen to the outside of either glass? Does this support your hypothesis? How does this show that when water vapor cools, it changes back to a liquid? What does this tell you about condensation?

Some places in the world have very little water on the ground or in the air. You may even live somewhere like that—in or near a desert, for example. This might affect your experiment. Can you explain why? If you didn't notice anything happening to either of your glasses, can you think of another experiment you could do to test your hypothesis?

Scientists often have to adapt their experiments to the circumstances. They may also have to run several experiments to confirm their results. Can you think of any more ways to test our original hypothesis? Would different experiments to test our hypothesis help us to be more certain that we reached an accurate conclusion? Now you're really starting to think like a scientist!

Experiment #4 Water on the Move

↖ Oceans, clouds, and rain are all part of Earth's water cycle.

Let's use what we know about condensation in another experiment. How does water move from a lake on the ground, to clouds in the sky, to rain falling to the ground, and then back again? That is, how does water move through the water cycle? If water vapor turns to liquid water when cooled, could liquid water become water vapor when heated?

Let's make this our hypothesis: **A process of evaporation, or the heating of liquid water into water vapor, and condensation, which involves the cooling of water vapor, is how water moves through the water cycle.**

Here's what you'll need:
- A small plastic or paper cup
- Warm water
- A resealable plastic bag
- Strong tape
- A sunny window

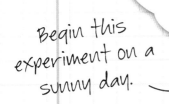

Begin this experiment on a sunny day.

Instructions:

This experiment will last two days. Remember that in order to answer questions, scientists sometimes set up experiments that take weeks, months, or even years to complete!

Be careful not to spill any water when you are taping the bag to the window.

1. Day 1: Fill ⅔ of your cup with warm water. Draw a line on the cup to mark the water level.

2. Carefully place the cup in the plastic bag so it stays upright. You may need to place the cup in a corner of the plastic bag and tilt the bag so the cup doesn't spill. Seal the bag, and tape it to a sunny window. Make sure no water spills and the cup remains upright.

3. Record the time, the day, and the details of the experiment. Be sure to include where the water is and how full the cup is. Check on the cup occasionally, recording the time, day, and observation.

4. Day 2: 24 hours after you started the experiment, come back to your bag. Where is the water level in the cup now? Has it changed? Why?

5. **Conclusion:**

How does this experiment show how water travels between the ground, the air, the sky, and back again? The bag represents the water cycle in nature. The sun served as a heat source. What does the water in the cup represent? If you said; "a body of water," you're right! As the sun heats the water in the cup, it turns into water vapor. Are there water droplets in the bag? Why? The vapor cools as it comes into contact with the walls of the bag.

In nature, vapor in the sky forms clouds. Water vapor in clouds cools and becomes rain or other precipitation. The condensed water then falls back to Earth. Some water returns to bodies of water. Some water falls to the soil, where plant roots absorb it. Eventually, those plants return the water to the air in the form of water vapor. It's an amazing system, isn't it?

Water is really old. It's nearly as old as planet Earth. That means the water you drink today could be the same water a dinosaur drank millions of years ago! This is because the water cycle never stops. Water is always evaporating, condensing, and falling as rain, snow, or hail. The water that falls collects in lakes, rivers, and oceans. Water repeats these actions over and over just as it has throughout the ages.

Experiment #5
The Power of Water

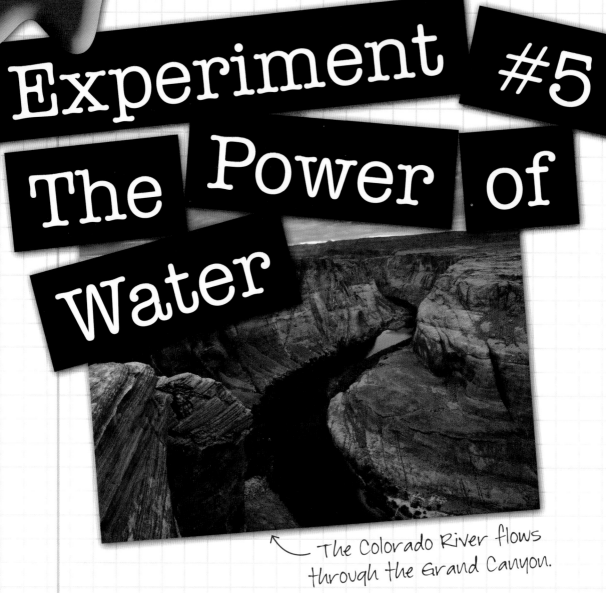

← The Colorado River flows through the Grand Canyon.

The water cycle has an effect on Earth itself. Over time, rain can wear mountains down to hills. Rivers can carve enormous canyons out of flat ground. Ocean waves can break rocks down to sand. This process of water breaking things down and carrying them away is called erosion.

To understand how erosion works, let's create our own mini-landscape and test the effects of water on it. You can be very creative with this experiment. In fact, with one setup, you can test many different hypotheses!

Pick one of these two possible hypotheses:

Hypothesis #1: Bare ground will erode faster than ground with rocks on it or with trees growing in the soil.

Hypothesis #2: Ground with rocks on it or trees growing in the soil will erode faster than bare ground.

Here's what you'll need:
- A paint roller pan or aluminum foil baking pan propped up on one side
- 2 paper or plastic cups
- Pebbles and small rocks of different sizes
- Small plants with roots, moss, and leaves
- Water
- Soil
- A knife

Be sure to ask for permission before digging up any plants!

Instructions:

1. Begin by creating a "landscape." At the high end of the pan, build soil up about 2 inches (5 centimeters) deep all the way across.

2. Use the knife to carefully punch holes evenly in the bottom of 1 cup. Fill the other cup with water. Hold the cup with holes over the high end of the pan.

3. Slowly pour the water into the cup with holes, sprinkling water evenly across the soil like rain. Let the water drain to the low end of the pan. Does anything happen or change in the landscape? What color is the water that collects in the low end of the pan? Why? Record all your observations.

4. Empty the pan and discard the wet soil. Using new soil, rebuild the landscape so it's exactly the same as the first time. This time, add pebbles and

Build a soil hill in the pan.

rocks to the landscape. Place them evenly across the side of the dirt slope.

5. Use the cups again to create "rain" over the pan. Is the result any different? What does the soil around the rocks look like? What color is the water that collects? Write down everything you see.

6. Once more, empty the pan, discard the wet soil, and rebuild the landscape using new soil. Add the plants to represent trees. Make sure the roots of the plants are in the soil. Gently press some leaves and moss into the soil, too. Use the cups to make rain again, and record all your observations.

Conclusion:

Which setup washed away the most dirt? Was the water more or less muddy when you put rocks in the soil? Did the rocks seem to keep the soil more stable? What about the plants? What do your results tell you about the relationship between plant cover and soil erosion?

Plants have an important connection to soil. Plants help slow down the flow of water as it passes over land. Plant roots act like a web that holds the soil in place. Roots help prevent soil from being washed away. Does this information help explain your results? Was your hypothesis correct?

Don't stop experimenting yet! What other ways could you change the landscape to continue testing

Erosion can create interesting shapes in rocks.

your hypothesis? What if you placed "trees" on only one side of your landscape, leaving the other side bare? Or placed trees on one side and made a "meadow" on the other by pressing moss, leaves, and grass into the soil?

What about the pan itself? What if you propped it up higher so the slope was steeper? What if you used different kinds of soils? Or changed how much rain fell or how hard? Could you make a river in your pan? What do you think would happen to the banks of your river if they were bare, had rocks, or were covered in trees?

Experiment #6

Do It Yourself!

Okay, scientists! Now you know many new things about water. You conducted experiments and made observations. In the last experiment, you learned how one experiment can raise and answer lots of different questions.

What else are you curious about when it comes to water? Have you ever wondered how natural bodies of water stay so clean? Or how freshwater and salt water differ? How plants lift water from the soil to their leaves? Can you think of anything else that interests you about water? Turn your questions into hypotheses, and test them for yourself.

You can do many kinds of experiments with water!

GLOSSARY

conclusion (kuhn-KLOO-zhuhn) a final decision, thought, or opinion

condensation (kahn-den-SAY-shuhn) the process in which a gas changes to a liquid or solid

displaces (diss-PLAYS-ez) takes the place of something or someone else

erosion (i-ROE-zhuhn) a gradual eating or wearing away by wind, water, or glaciers

evaporation (i-vah-puh-RAY-shuhn) the process in which a liquid changes to a gas

hypothesis (hy-POTH-uh-sihss) a logical guess about what will happen in an experiment

method (METH-uhd) a way of doing something

molecules (MOL-uh-kyoolz) the smallest parts of a substance that still have the chemical properties of that substance

observations (ob-zur-VAY-shuhnz) things that are seen or noticed with one's senses

precipitation (pri-sih-puh-TAY-shuhn) rain, snow, sleet, or hail that falls toward the surface of Earth

water vapor (WAH-ter VAY-per) water in its gas state

FOR MORE INFORMATION

BOOKS

Kalman, Bobbie. *The Water Cycle*. New York: Crabtree Publishing Company, 2006.

Royston, Angela. *The Life and Times of a Drop of Water*. Chicago: Raintree, 2006.

Strauss, Rochelle. *One Well: The Story of Water on Earth*. Toronto: Kids Can Press, 2007.

WEB SITES

Droplet and the Water Cycle

kids.earth.nasa.gov/droplet.html

A fun online game about the water cycle from the National Aeronautics and Space Administration (NASA)

EPA Environmental Kids Club—Water

www.epa.gov/kids/water.htm

A collection of fun activities that teach you more about water

USGS: The Water Cycle—For Kids

ga.water.usgs.gov/edu/watercycleplacemat.html

A fun diagram from the U.S. Geological Survey explaining the water cycle

INDEX

About the Authors

Charnan Simon is a former editor of *Cricket* magazine and the author of more than 100 books for young readers. She lives in Seattle, Washington, where there is a lot of water.

Ariel Kazunas is writer who has worked for several nonprofit magazines. She is also a kayak guide and instructor, which explains her love of all things having to do with water. This is her first book for young readers.